Contents

Introduction

Reaching Up

Reaching In

Group's Best Discussion Launchers

for Youth ministry

Group
Loveland, Colorado

Group's Best Discussion Launchers for Youth Ministry

Copyright © 1997 Group Publishing, Inc.

Credits
Editor: Helen Turnbull
Managing Editor: Michael D. Warden
Chief Creative Officer: Joani Schultz
Copy Editor: Pamela Shoup
Art Director: Lisa Chandler
Assistant Art Director: Bill Fisher
Cover Art Director: Helen H. Lannis
Computer Graphic Artist: Anne Vetter
Cover Designer: Diana Walters
Cover Photography: FPG International
Production Manager: Gingar Kunkel

Unless otherwise noted, Scriptures quoted from The Youth Bible, New Century Version, copyright © 1991 by Word Publishing, Dallas, Texas 75039. Used by permission.

Library of Congress Cataloging-in-Publication Data
Group's best discussion launchers for youth ministry.
       p.   cm.
   Includes index
   ISBN 0-7644-2023-2
   1. Church group work with teenagers.   I. Group Publishing.
BV4447.G6945   1997
268'.433—dc21   96-48438
                                    CIP

10 9 8 7 6 5 4 3 2 1   06 05 04 03 02 01 00 99 98 97

Printed in the United States of America.

Introduction

OK, so let's talk shop. You could use some extra help with your youth group. Your meetings are going well, but they could use a little zing. Maybe the activity you have planned is turning out to be a yawner. Perhaps there's a sensitive topic you need to discuss, and you don't know where to start. Or maybe your class has simply gotten out of control. You've tried everything, and you're running out of ideas. How are you going to connect?

Teenagers today face a lot of serious issues: abortion, AIDS, war, cults, gangs, and suicide. Yet they still struggle with the problems that challenge every young generation: dating, parents, school, self-image, and popularity. Here are "in-your-face" discussions that'll help you connect with your youth group and teach them how to trust God, even with the most difficult problems.

Group's Best Discussion Launchers for Youth Ministry is a compilation of some of our best and most important discussion activities to help your teenagers make the right decisions. Section one, "Reaching Up," deals with questions your kids might ask about God's power and how it relates to them. Teach your kids how to find their identity in Christ with the lessons from section two, "Reaching In." Finally, section three, "Reaching Out," helps your teenagers realize their impact on others. These lessons will prepare you with topics that teenagers often avoid and will give you compelling discussion questions that steer kids to look inside themselves.

Some lessons start with a quick activity; others simply include a set of catalytic quotes guaranteed to generate reaction. Each topic correlates with a point to keep your discussion in focus. The activities require little or no supplies; at most, all you'll need are Bibles, pencils or pens, paper, newsprint, markers, tape, index cards, and other classroom items. Also, keep in mind that the time frames listed with the activities are estimates; you'll be surprised at how carried away your students will get with a topic that hits close to home.

Be prepared: This book deals with some pretty sensitive issues. It's a tough job, but with a little help, you can do it. Don't forget to enjoy, encourage, and energize. Be creative, but be sensitive also. Most of all, take time to revel in watching the positive effect you'll have on your kids' spiritual growth.

Reaching Up

REACHING UP REACHING UP
REACHING UP REACHING UP
REACHING UP REACHING UP
REACHING UP REACHING UP
REACHING UP REACHING UP
REACHING UP REACHING UP
REACHING UP REACHING UP
REACHING UP REACHING UP

☞Direct Link

> **TOPIC:** Abundant Life
> **THE POINT:** Jesus brings abundant life today.
> **TIME:** 5 to 10 minutes

Call kids together, and say: **We're going to play a quick game of Tag.** Have one student volunteer to be "It." (If you have more than fifteen kids in your class, form two groups and have two games going at the same time.) Say: **The object of the game is to avoid being tagged. If someone tags you, you're out and must sit down. But you can get back in the game if someone who isn't It links arms with you. When you're linked with someone, you and your partner are safe for the rest of the game (but you can only link with someone who's already out of the game— you can't start the game linked together). If you haven't been tagged and see someone sitting down, try to link arms with that person so he or she can play the game again. Ready? Go!**

After two minutes, stop the game, have someone else volunteer to be It, and start the game over. When kids have played for two more minutes, have them form (or stay in) pairs to discuss the following questions.

discussion questions

● What was it like to sit down while others played the game?
● What was it like to play the game after becoming a pair with another player?
● How was playing this game like living in our world without Jesus?
● How was playing the game with a partner like living our lives with Jesus?
● What can you do this week to learn more about the abundant life Jesus wants to give you?

☞What's the Story?

TOPIC: The Bible

THE POINT: The Bible is the most incredible book you could ever read.

TIME: 10 to 15 minutes

Have kids form trios. Give each student paper and a pencil. Say: **As a trio, write a story. Assign one person to write the beginning of your story, another to write the middle, and another to write the ending. However, you cannot work together to create your story. Each person must write his or her part of the story alone. You can't talk or write notes to each other to find out what your partners are creating. Just sit with your backs together and write your assigned parts of the story. You have three minutes.**

After three minutes, have kids finish their writing, and have each trio read its story aloud and in order—beginning, middle, and ending. While each trio reads its story, have students from other trios act it out.

After all trios have read their stories, direct them to discuss these questions:

discussion questions

● What's your reaction to hearing your story? to telling it to others?

● How is creating your story like the way God created the Bible? How is it different?

● The Bible was written by many different people, but it tells one unified story. Based on what you've learned from this activity, will you change how you study the Bible? Why or why not?

● Do you think the Bible is the most incredible book you could ever read? Why or why not?

☞**In a Perfect World**

TOPIC: Creation
THE POINT: God created the universe.
TIME: 10 to 15 minutes

Say: **If you could create the perfect planet to live on, what would it be like? Think of your answer to this question right now, and create characteristics of your planet— its name, inhabitants, and natural laws, such as whether the planet has a gravitational pull. For example, if you like music, maybe your planet would have singing trees or music playing every time your feet touch the ground.**

After students have invented their own planets, have each student find an object in the room that best represents his or her planet. For example, if a person's planet has light all day long, the person's object could be a light bulb.

Then have each student find a partner. Tell partners to show each other the objects they chose and explain why the objects represent their planets. When pairs have finished, have them discuss the following questions.

discussion questions

- What was it like to create your own planet?
- Why did you create your planet the way you did?
- What was it like to find an object to represent your planet?
- How was the way you "created" your planet like the way God created the universe? How was it different?
- Why do you think God created the universe as it is?
- Do you think God could choose an object to represent his creation? Why or why not? If so, what might he choose?

☞Don't Give Up!

> **TOPIC:** Endurance
> **THE POINT:** The Holy Spirit encourages and helps you.
> **TIME:** 10 to 15 minutes

Have kids form two teams. (If you have twenty or more students, have kids form two groups and play two sets of the game at the same time.) Have teams each form a single file line facing you.

Say: **We're going to play a game. The object is to think of ways we can encourage and help each other. But there's a twist. The first person in line on one team will think of a way to encourage or help someone, shout it out, and run to the back of his or her line. The first person on the second team must start acting out that encouragement. For example, if someone shouts out "listen," you could cup your hand around your ear. However, while you're making that motion you also have to think of another way to encourage or help someone, such as writing an encouraging note, and shout it out. Then run to the back of your line. The second person in the first line must start acting out your idea and thinking of another one to shout out. Teams keep doing this until one team is stumped or repeats a way to encourage or help people that either team has already said.**

When students understand the game, have them begin. After playing a few rounds of the game, have kids form pairs to discuss the following questions.

discussion questions

● How are some of the ways we encourage and help others like the ways the Holy Spirit encourages and helps us? How are they different?

● How did it feel to play this game in a team?

● How was playing this game in a team like the

way the Holy Spirit encourages and helps you? How was it different?

● Have you ever felt encouraged or helped by the Holy Spirit? Explain.

● What's one thing you can do in the coming week to allow the Holy Spirit to encourage and help you?

☞Zero In

TOPIC: Evolution
THE POINT: God created the universe.
TIME: 10 to 15 minutes

Form two teams. Give each team ten coins, and have them lay the coins on the floor. Have teams form a circle around their coins. Say: **Let's have a contest to see which team can flip their coins so they come up all "heads." Flip the coins one at a time until you've flipped them all. If they don't all come up heads, keep flipping them until they do. The first team to come up with all heads wins.**

Allow kids to continue until they grow tired of the activity, then stop the action and ask:

● **What do you think the odds are of getting all ten coins to come up heads?** (Answer: 1 in 4,132,800.)

● **How does that make you feel about this activity?**

● **Compared to the odds in this activity, what's the probability of a single amino acid chain—the smallest string known in a living thing—forming by chance?**

After several kids guess, give them each paper and pencils and have them start writing zeros. On your own sheet of paper, write, "1 in 10000 . . . " and fill your page with zeros. Once kids have filled their pages, have them count the number of zeros they wrote and jot this number on the back of the paper. Collect the papers, then tape them together in a row, with yours at the left end, until you have created a number that starts with "1" and is followed by 240 zeros. Tell kids that this number represents the probability of even simple life happening by chance on earth.

Then have kids discuss the following questions.

discussion questions

- What's your reaction to this number?
- How does this probability make you feel about evolution? creationism?
- Does this fact convince you that God created the universe? Why or why not?

☞Lift Me Up

TOPIC: Faith
THE POINT: You can trust God.
SCRIPTURE: John 10:27-29 and 1 Peter 5:7
TIME: 10 to 15 minutes

Have students form groups of three. Distribute pencil and paper and ask each group to brainstorm, listing eight to ten things that they worry about. After a few minutes, say: **Hand the list to one person in your group, then the other two of you pick up that person. You'll be holding him or her for a while, so get as comfortable as you can.** Make sure that the two students are standing, and that the third student is completely off the floor. If you don't have enough students to form groups of three, they may work in pairs, with one partner carrying the other.
Ask:

discussion questions

- How is holding your group member like carrying your worries and stress?
- How do you feel holding your group member?
- How long do you think you could hold your group member?

Say: **You can put your group member down, but listen while I read John 10:27-29 and 1 Peter 5:7.** Read the verses, then ask:

- How do you deal with stress? For example,

do you keep your stress inside or do you allow others to help you with it?

● Do you believe that Jesus is able to deal with your worries? Why or why not?

● How do you feel knowing that Jesus holds you in his hand?

● What can you do to give your worries to him?

Say: **Because he cares for you, you can trust God to deal with anything that worries you. In your groups, pray together over the worries on your list. Hold your fists clenched as you say each worry, imagining that you are holding it in your hand. Unclench your fists and let it go as you ask God to take care of it.**

☞ The Meaning of Life

TOPIC: The Future

THE POINT: God's Spirit reveals your true purpose in life.

SCRIPTURE: Ephesians 5:15-17

TIME: 5 to 10 minutes

Form pairs so kids can discuss their reactions to these quotes:

"You have to intertwine God's will in your life with what you want to do also. You can't just live God's life, ya know."
—Walls1Door, in a discussion on religion, from America Online

"I consider myself a good person, and I have my own set of what I believe are well-rounded morals. I can't live my life always thinking of what God would want me to do in each situation. I've got to be independent."
—Navi14, in the same discussion, from America Online

"So be very careful how you live. Do not live like those who are not wise, but live wisely. Use every chance you have for doing good, because these are evil times. So do not be foolish but learn what the Lord wants you to do."

—the Apostle Paul, from Ephesians 5:15-17

discussion questions

- What's your reaction to the first two quotes?
- How do you think Paul's words in Ephesians apply to what the other people said?
- What do you think Paul would say to these people if he were here?
- What would you say to them?
- Since we know that God's Spirit reveals our true purpose in life, how can we follow Paul's advice and "learn what the Lord wants [us] to do"?
- Is following God's Spirit the same as being wise? Why or why not?
- Do you follow God's Spirit? Why or why not?

☞Hard to Be Humble

TOPIC: Humility
THE POINT: God is holy.
TIME: 10 to 15 minutes

Have kids form pairs so they can discuss their reactions to the following poem.

Mercy
For years I've walked the "narrow trail"
So casual the love
So hollow the heart
that beats in mockery to Your Holiness
I sense it like a stench from Hell itself,
invading me to wrench Your love away. . .

My God!
Your ways are not like mine.
—Michael D. Warden

discussion questions

● What's your reaction to the poem?
● What do you think the poem's author was expressing about himself? about God?
● How would understanding God's holiness help you understand this poem?
● Do you think the author is expressing true humility? Why or why not?
● If you wrote a poem or letter to God about his holiness or your own humility, would it differ from this poem? If so, how?

After the discussion distribute paper and pencils, and ask each person to write a poem or letter to God. The poems can express their feelings about God's holiness, asking him to help the whole group grow in humility. When kids are finished, challenge them to keep the prayers in their Bibles and pray them to God every day for the next week.

☞Heroic Measures

TOPIC: Idolatry
THE POINT: We're created with the need to worship.
TIME: 5 to 10 minutes

Have kids form pairs so they can discuss their reactions to these quotes.

"I don't understand why people would buy one sneaker endorsed by one player over the other. Kids idolize professional athletes, which is wrong in itself, and they just copy what they're wearing . . . To kids that idolize me, I tell them don't do so just because I can dribble a basketball—that's really sick."

—Charles Barkley, professional basketball player
(*The Performance Illusion* by Chap Clark)

"Worship is dangerous. It is not a retreat from reality, but a direct engagement with ultimate reality: God. Genuine worship is a response to God and what he has done; in it we make ourselves vulnerable to the story of Israel and Jesus. Does anyone have the foggiest idea what sort of power we so blithely invoke? The churches are children playing on the floor with their chemistry sets, mixing up a batch of TNT to kill a Sunday morning. It is madness to wear ladies' straw hats and velvet hats to church; we should all be wearing crash helmets. Ushers should issue life preservers and signal flares; they should lash us to our pews."

—Annie Dillard, author

(Quoted in *People of the Truth*, excerpted by Chap Clark in *The Performance Illusion*)

discussion questions

● What's your reaction to Charles Barkley's quote?

- Why do you think some people idolize professional athletes?
- What's your reaction to what Annie Dillard says worship should be like?
- How is her description like your worship experiences? How is it different?
- How do these quotes express that we're created with the need to worship?
- Based on these quotes, which would you rather worship: God or something else?
- Why do you think God wants us to focus on him and not on other things or people?
- Do you think we were created with the need to worship? Why or why not?
- What do you worship? Explain.
- How can you make God the number one focus in your life?

☞ And Justice for All

TOPIC: Injustice

THE POINT: God's justice will never fail you.

TIME: 5 to 10 minutes

Have kids form trios to discuss their reactions to these quotes:

"No person shall . . . be deprived of life, liberty, or property, without due process of law; nor shall private property be taken for public use, without just compensation."

—excerpted from Amendment 5 of the United States Constitution

"Federal and state officials now have the power to seize your business, home, bank account, records and personal property ... Everything you have can be taken away at the whim of one or two federal or state officials. Regardless of sex, age, race or economic situation, we are all potential victims."

—Rep. Henry J. Hyde
("Guilty until proven innocent," USA Today, July 11, 1995)

discussion questions

- What's your reaction to these quotes?
- Do you believe the government is fair? Why or why not?
- Do you believe God is fair? Why or why not?
- Is God fair if he allows the government to take your possessions or hurt you in any way? Why or why not?
- Do you believe that God's actions will always seem fair to you? Why or why not?
- Do you believe that God's justice will never fail you?
- What's the difference between fairness and justice?

☞What if God Was One of Us?

TOPIC: Jesus
THE POINT: God became human for you.
SCRIPTURE: John 3:16
TIME: 5 to 10 minutes

Have kids form pairs. Use the discussion questions below to get kids' reactions to these quotes:

"I don't know what the big deal is about Jesus. He was some great leader, right? So was Gandhi. So was Hitler, for that matter."
—Anonymous Internet surfer

"God loved the world so much that he gave his one and only Son so that whoever believes in him may not be lost, but have eternal life."
—Jesus, from John 3:16

discussion questions

- Do you agree with the first quote? Why or why not?
- How *is* Jesus different from other leaders?
- When people began to reject God, God could have simply changed their hearts. Instead, he became human, like us, in Jesus. What do you think caused God to choose that option?
- What does God's decision to become human say about how he feels about you?

☞Giving Thanks

TOPIC: Jesus' Power
THE POINT: Jesus died on the cross for you.
TIME: 5 to 10 minutes

Have kids form pairs, and say: **Turn to your partner, and tell that person the nicest thing you've ever done for someone else, such as comforting a sibling when he or she was depressed or throwing a surprise birthday party for a friend.**

After everyone has shared, invite students to tell the class what their partners did for others. Then have partners discuss these questions:

discussion questions

- Of all the nice things people in this room have done for others, which do you think was the nicest? Why?
- What were you thinking and feeling as you did a nice thing for someone else? What was that person's response to you?

Then have partners share the nicest thing someone has done for each of them. After everyone has shared, invite pairs to tell their stories to the rest of the class. Then have partners discuss these questions.

- Of all the nice things others have done for people in this group, which do you think was the best? Why?
- What was your reaction when someone did something nice for you? How did you respond to that person?
- How do you feel about the fact that Jesus died on the cross for you? How does that make you want to respond to him?

☞In Search of...

TOPIC: Jesus' Resurrection

THE POINT: Jesus really rose from the dead.

TIME: 15 to 20 minutes

Have kids form three groups. Say: **Your job is to stage the disappearance of one of your group members. You not only have to make the person disappear from the room, you have to create a story about how that person disappeared. Your person must stay on the grounds but** can hide anywhere inside or outside the building. You have five minutes to complete the disappearance and create your story about it.

After five minutes, have everyone gather back together. Have groups tell their stories of how their "disappearing" members vanished. Then begin a search for the missing people, with each group looking for the members from the two other groups. The first group to find another group's person wins.

When all three disappearing members have been found, have kids form pairs within their groups to discuss these questions:

discussion questions

● How did you feel trying to explain how your group member disappeared?

● Disappearing members, what was it like to hide and wait for someone to find you?

● Which of the three stories was most believable to you? Why?

● How were the disappearances of each group member like Jesus' resurrection? How were they different?

● What part of Jesus' resurrection is most difficult for you to believe? Why?

● What part is easiest for you to believe? Why?

● How does this activity affect your beliefs about Jesus rising from the dead?

☞Eye Opener

TOPIC: Love

THE POINT: Jesus loves us more than life itself.

SCRIPTURE: John 3:16

TIME: 10 to 15 minutes

Have kids scatter throughout the room. Say: **Close your eyes. When I say "go," start walking around the room** without talking. Keep your eyes closed the entire time. You might bump into someone or something, so walk slowly to avoid getting hurt. If you do have a collision, turn and walk in another direction. Ready? Go!

As kids begin to walk, open your Bible to John 3:16. Tap one student on the shoulder, and whisper: **You may open your eyes.** Hand that student your Bible, then say: **Read John 3:16 to yourself. Then tap someone else on the shoulder and instruct that person to open his or her eyes, read the verse, and pass the Bible to someone else. Then sit down.** If you have more Bibles, tap other students and give them the same instructions.

When everyone has read the verse and sat down, have kids form pairs to discuss the following questions.

discussion questions

● What were you thinking as you walked with your eyes closed? as you read the Bible verse? as you sat with your eyes open?

● How were you feeling throughout this activity?

● How was this activity like looking for love? How was it different?

● Have you ever felt lost and unloved? If so, when? How did you handle it?

● What did you learn about God's love for you through this activity?

● Now that you know more about God's love for you, what will you do about it?

Say: **When we look for love in other people, it's like walking around with our eyes closed. Human love is imperfect, and even when people mean well, we're bound to get hurt. But Jesus loves us more than life itself. His love is perfect. When we accept his love, it's like opening our eyes and seeing where we're walking. We can experience love without fearing we'll get hurt.**

Within your pairs, pray that your partner will know and experience true love in Jesus Christ. You may pray silently if you wish.

☞Fruit of the Vine

TOPIC: New Age Movement
THE POINT: Real spiritual growth means becoming more like Jesus.
SCRIPTURE: John 15:5-13
TIME: 5 to 10 minutes

Form groups of three or four to discuss their reactions to these quotes from the book *Ask Me If I Care* by Nancy Rubin.

"I don't believe in hell or heaven exactly, but I see death simply as a transition between life on earth and life in some other existence or plane. I believe most strongly in reincarnation, that you come back to earth for whatever number of lives it takes to learn all you can from the earth."
—Female, age 15

"I cannot name what I believe in, it has no name. It is the total awareness of everything, it is the guide that brought about the beauty of the earth. . . It is the shape of a rock or the shape of a thought. . .I feel a large part of it is nature, but I will never be sure. It helps to have it there."
—Male, age 16

discussion questions

● What's your reaction to these teenagers' comments?
● If these young people were here right now, what would you tell them is your belief about real spirituality?
● If real spiritual growth means becoming

more like Jesus, is it possible for these two teenagers to really grow spiritually? Why or why not?
- What's the best way for a teenager to grow spiritually?
- How do you think Jesus would answer the previous question?

Close by reading aloud John 15:5-13.

☞ The Spirit Around You

TOPIC: Paranormal Experiences
THE POINT: The spiritual realm is all around you.
SCRIPTURE: Ezekiel 1:15-18
TIME: 10 to 15 minutes

Have a volunteer read aloud Ezekiel 1:15-18. Give each person a sheet of paper and a pencil. Have kids put their papers on their heads and try to draw the "wheel within the wheel" as described in Ezekiel.

When kids finish, have them look at their masterpieces. Say: **It might be easier to draw the wheels if your paper were in front of you, but that's because you're used to that perspective. Just as it must've been hard for Ezekiel to explain what he saw, so it's hard for us to see and understand things going on in the spiritual realm.**

Read aloud this description of a UFO sighting, then discuss the questions on page 26.

It was a large, round object that descended over us and hovered about fifty feet above our car. There was a row of lights around the edge that circled like tracer lights in a clockwise motion. Near the center of the craft, another row of lights traced around in the opposite direction. Many other lights speckled the bottom of the craft in a random pattern. After it hovered over us for a few minutes, the craft jerked away quickly. It paused

momentarily and jerked quickly into another direction and then accelerated until it disappeared.

discussion questions

● How is this account of a UFO sighting similar to the description in Ezekiel 1:15-18? How is it different?

● What do you think Ezekiel saw?

● How do these two experiences demonstrate that the spiritual realm is all around us?

● How might knowing that the spiritual realm is all around you impact the way you live?

☞ Listen Up!

> **TOPIC:** Prayer
>
> **THE POINT:** God communicates our answers to prayers in many different ways.
>
> **TIME:** 5 to 10 minutes

Have kids form pairs. Have each pair designate one person as the "Talker" and the other as the "Un-listener." Say: **Talkers, you have one minute to talk about the best day of your life. Un-listeners, do whatever it takes to *not* listen, such as covering your ears, humming, or turning away from the Talker. Ready, go!**

After one minute, have students switch roles and repeat the activity for another minute.

When the second turn is over, have pairs discuss the following questions:

discussion questions

● How did you feel during this experience?

● When do you feel like someone's not listening to you? Explain.

● Do you think God listens to your prayers? Why or why not?

- Do you listen to God's answers to your prayers? Why or why not?
- How is this experience like the way you listen to God?

☞Reign on Me

TOPIC: Priorities

THE POINT: You can be ready for Christ's return.

SCRIPTURE: Romans 13:11-14

TIME: 10 to 15 minutes

Form groups of four. Assign each group member one of these roles to report on: teachers, parents, friends, and the media. Then say: **In your group, answer this question for the role you've been assigned—What do your** (teachers, parents, friends, the media) **seem to think your priorities should be?**

After kids have discussed this question for each of their assigned roles, form four new groups, with all those reporting on teachers in one group, on parents in a second, and so on. Have the four groups come together to form four lines in an X shape, with kids facing the center of the X. (If your meeting room is small, move to a larger area or outside.)

Say: **Now we're going to have a four-way Tug of War. The four people at the front of the lines (those in the center of the room) need to lock arms. The rest of you, put your arms around the waist of the person in front of you. When I give the signal, try to pull the other three groups into your corner of the room. And while you're pulling, I want each of you to keep shouting out one or more of the priorities from parents, teachers, friends, or the media that your group discussed.**

Give the signal and let kids pull. After several seconds, stop the Tug of War and discuss the following questions.

discussion questions

- What was the atmosphere in this room when we

were pulling and shouting out the different priorities?

● How is that like real life for you?

Read aloud Romans 13:11-14, then have kids return to their foursomes to discuss these questions:

● Based on this passage, what priorities do you sometimes choose that are contrary to God's priorities?

● If we all tried to live so that we were ready for Christ's return instead of just satisfying ourselves (verse 14), how would our daily priorities change?

☞Standing Strong

> **TOPIC:** Rebellion
>
> **THE POINT:** Jesus is a "holy rebel" you can follow.
>
> **SCRIPTURE:** Ephesians 6:10-13
>
> **TIME:** 10 to 15 minutes

Form groups of five or more. If you have fewer than ten people, just keep students together in one group.

Choose one volunteer from each group to be the "Rebel." Place each Rebel side by side, about two feet away from the wall. Ask Rebels to lean forward and brace their bodies against the wall by placing one foot in front of the other and resting their palms against the wall. Make sure Rebels lock their arms.

When all the Rebels are in place, say to the groups: **Your job is to line up single file behind your Rebel and work as a group to try to push him or her straight into the wall. You can touch only the shoulders of the person in front of you. You have one minute. Go!**

While kids are straining, read aloud Ephesians 6:10-13. After one minute, call time. Gather kids and ask these questions:

discussion questions

● How were the Rebels in this experience like rebels in real life?
● How is Jesus like our Rebels?

Read aloud Ephesians 6:10-13 again. Then ask:

● What does this passage have to say about positive rebellion?
● Why was it so difficult for your group to push the Rebel into the wall, even though the group was stronger?
● How is that like the strength that comes from following God in a positive rebellion against sin?

Read aloud Ephesians 6:10-13 a third time and ask kids each to share a time when they stood their ground effectively for all the right reasons.

☞Work in Progress

TOPIC: School
THE POINT: You always represent God.
TIME: 5 to 10 minutes

Give each student a sheet of paper and a pencil. Write at the top of a sheet of paper "PBPWMGINFWMY."

Hold up the paper, point to what you've written, and say: **Pop quiz! You have one minute to write down what this means.**

After a minute, invite students to share their answers to the quiz. Then say: **This word represents the sentence "Please be patient with me—God is not finished with me yet."**

Have kids form small groups to discuss the following questions.

discussion questions

- How did you feel when I declared a pop quiz?
- If you were really getting a grade on this quiz, what would you do to get the right answer? Why?
- Would you represent God well in the way you tried to get the right answer? Why or why not?
- If God called a pop quiz on how you represent him at school, what grade would you get? Why?
- How might the sentence "Please be patient with me—God is not finished with me yet" apply to how you represent God?
- What are some different ways you can represent God at school? What's one way you could represent God at school in the coming week?
- How might these actions affect your life at school? outside of school?

☞Facing the Real Enemy

TOPIC: Spiritual Warfare
THE POINT: Spiritual forces are at work in your life.
TIME: 5 to 10 minutes

Have kids form pairs to discuss their reactions to the following quote:

"In the mailbag at the U.S. attorney's office in Boise on Feb. 7, 1991, were letters addressed to the office's 13 lawyers, but only one was addressed to the 'Servant of Queen of Babylon.'"

"For Maurice Ellsworth, the U.S. attorney for Idaho, it was one of the strangest letters he'd ever seen. It said the stink of lawless government had reached 'Yahweh' and 'Yashua.' 'Whether we live or whether we die,' the letter read, 'we will not bow to your evil commandments.' It was dated Feb. 3, 1991, mailed from a P.O. Box in Naples, Idaho, and signed Mrs. Vicki Weaver.

"U.S. marshals quickly found out Vicki Weaver was the wife of a guy who'd recently been arrested on a charge of selling sawed-off shotguns without a federal permit. They found out that Weaver had been a difficult arrest, and that he had vowed not to be arrested again. Weaver was a survivalist; he and his family lived in a cabin in isolated Ruby Ridge, and at the edge of their property stood a painted plywood sign: 'Every knee shall bow to Yashua Messiah.'"

(Source: "What Went Wrong at Ruby Ridge," Newsweek, August 28, 1995.)

discussion questions

● What's your reaction to this quote?
● How does your view of spiritual warfare differ from Vicki Weaver's view?
● What would you say to Vicki and her family if they were here?
● How would you answer somebody who said only wackos believe spiritual forces are real and at work in our lives?
● Do you believe spiritual forces are at work in your life? Why or why not?

☞Heart, Soul, and Strength

TOPIC: The Trinity

THE POINT: God's character never changes.

SCRIPTURE: Deuteronomy 6:4-5

TIME: 5 to 10 minutes

Have kids form pairs to discuss their reactions to this quote:

> "Hear, O Israel: The Lord our God, the Lord is one. Love the Lord your God with all your heart and with all your soul and with all your strength."
>
> —Deuteronomy 6:4-5, New International Version

discussion questions

● This Scripture represents the heart of Jewish thought about God. For Jews, it's also one of the biggest obstacles to accepting the Christian's Trinitarian view of God. Why do you think that's so?

● Do you think this passage rejects the possibility that God might express himself as Father, Son, and Holy Spirit? Why or why not?

● How does the fact that God's character never changes impact the way you see this passage? the way you see the Trinity?

● If you were asked to explain the Trinity to the entire Jewish community, what would you say?

● Do you think this passage describes your life? Why or why not?

● How would your life change if you lived every day according to the command in this passage?

☞ Hand of Providence

> **TOPIC:** War
> **THE POINT:** Only God can bring lasting peace to the world.
> **TIME:** 5 to 10 minutes

Write on sheets of paper the following quotes about war and tape them to the wall. Have volunteers read the quotes aloud. Then have pairs discuss the following questions.

"All wars are boyish, and are fought by boys."
—Herman Melville, 1866

"It is easier to lead men to combat and to stir up their passions than to temper them and urge them to the patient labors of peace."
—André Gide, 1938

"We think—although of course, now, we very seldom clearly think—that the other side of war is peace."
—Edna St. Vincent Millay, 1940

"In the final choice a soldier's pack is not so heavy a burden as a prisoner's chains."
—Dwight D. Eisenhower, 1953

"Youth is the first victim of war; the first fruit of peace. It takes 20 years or more of peace to make a man; it takes only 20 seconds of war to destroy him."

—Baudouin I of Belgium, 1959

discussion questions

- Which of these quotes do you agree with? Explain.
- Which of these quotes do you disagree with? Explain.
- Do any of these quotes relate to the notion that only God can bring lasting peace to the world? Why or why not?
- Which of these quotes relates to the struggle or battle we fight with sin?
- How does knowing that only God can bring lasting peace to the world affect the way you view war?

☞ Freeze Frame

TOPIC: Worship
THE POINT: You can worship God in everything you do.
TIME: 10 to 15 minutes

Call your students together, and say: **We're going to play a quick game. When I say "go," all of you will run around the room moving your bodies in different ways. For example, you might swing your arms, skip, crawl, or make faces. When I say "freeze," stop and hold your positions. Then I'll give you some more instructions. Ready? Go!**

After fifteen seconds, say: **Freeze! Now find a partner near you, and tell that person how you might worship God in the position you're in right now. For example, if you're bending over, you might be smelling a rose and thanking God for creating it.**

Allow kids some time to share, then play the game again. Play as many rounds as you'd like. Then have kids form foursomes to discuss these questions:

discussion questions

● How does this game reflect the idea that you can worship God in everything you do?

● Were you worshiping God as we played the game? Why or why not?

● If you were worshiping God during the game, how were you worshiping him?

● What are some recent "freeze frame" moments in your real life when you worshiped God?

● How can you worship God through things you'll be doing the rest of this day?

➤Reaching In

REACHING   IN   REACHING   IN
REACHING   IN   REACHING   IN
REACHING   IN   REACHING   IN
REACHING   IN   REACHING   IN
REACHING   IN   REACHING   IN
REACHING   IN   REACHING   IN
REACHING   IN   REACHING   IN
REACHING   IN   REACHING   IN

☞Action Packed

> **TOPIC:** Commitment
>
> **THE POINT:** When you commit to God, you grow spiritually.
>
> **TIME:** 10 to 15 minutes

Have kids form trios. Have trios brainstorm and make a list of things people commit to, such as playing a sport well, getting good grades, or being a good friend. Then have trios pick one commitment from their list and think of three actions someone would have to do to fulfill that commitment. For example, if someone committed to being a good basketball player, he or she might practice free throws, run, and watch professional basketball players on television. Have trios assign each member one action to perform.

When groups have finished, say: **We're going to play a game. I'll call trios up, one at a time. When your trio is in front, all three members will pantomime their actions at the same time. The rest of you must guess the commitment that the group is acting out.**

After each group has acted out its commitment, have trios discuss the following questions.

dicussion questions

- How would the actions each trio acted out help them meet the commitment they chose?
- What commitments have you made in your life?
- What actions do you take to fulfill your commitments?
- What have been the results of your commitments?
- What actions would you do to fulfill a commitment to God?
- What might be the results of those actions?
- Do you believe this statement: When you commit to God, you grow spiritually? Why or why not?

● What one action are you willing to do this week to grow closer to God?

☞ How to Be a Jesus Freak

TOPIC: Commitment
THE POINT: Your relationship with Jesus is worth suffering for.
SCRIPTURE: John 15:18-20 and Matthew 16:25-26
TIME: 5 to 10 minutes

Form groups of two or three to discuss kids' reactions to these quotes:

"Some people think there are no such things as Christian teenagers. We are afraid to speak out because we are constantly discriminated against by secular kids. Stop looking down on us because of our beliefs. The Bill of Rights applies to us too."

—Kimberly Priore, a fourteen-year-old from Massachusetts (Seventeen Magazine)

"Believe in me! Help me believe in anything. I want to be someone who believes."
—From the song "Mr. Jones" by Counting Crows

"Those who want to save their lives will give up true life, and those who give up their lives for me will have true life. It is worth nothing for them to have the whole world if they lose their souls."
—Jesus of Nazareth, from Matthew 16:25-26

discussion questions

- What's your reaction to these quotes?
- What would you say to Kimberly if she were in the room?
- What would you say to Jesus?

Read aloud John 15:18-20. Then ask:

- What do you think Jesus would say to Kimberly? to the Counting Crows?
- Who do you most closely identify with: Kimberly, Jesus, or the Counting Crows? Explain.
- Do you think your relationship with Jesus is worth suffering for? Why or why not?

☞ Grave Concerns

TOPIC: Death
THE POINT: Jesus defeated death for you.
SCRIPTURE: 2 Timothy 1:10b
TIME: 5 to 10 minutes

Form trios so kids can discuss their reactions to one or both of these quotes:

"[Teens] can understand the fact that death is permanent and that it will happen to everyone one day, however . . . they fantasize that death may be defied."

—Mary Fran Hazinki, excerpted by James Watkins in *Death & Beyond*

"[Jesus] destroyed death, and through the Good News he showed us the way to have life that cannot be destroyed."

—the Apostle Paul, from 2 Timothy 1:10b

discussion questions

- Do these quotes agree with each other? Why or why not?
- Which quote do you agree with more? Explain.
- Do you think there's a life that cannot be destroyed—even by death? Explain.
- If you believe you have a life in Christ that cannot be destroyed, are you still afraid of death? Why or why not?
- Why do you think Jesus defeated death for you? What was he trying to accomplish?
- How would your life change if you were absolutely convinced that Jesus defeated death for you?

☞Happily Ever After

TOPIC: Disappointment
THE POINT: God brings good out of suffering.
SCRIPTURE: Philippians 4:12b-13
TIME: 5 to 10 minutes

Form pairs so kids can discuss their reactions to one or both of the following quotes.

"It is possible to fall in love with your problems."

—Jim Long

("Surprised by Joy," Campus Life, February 1996)

"I have learned the secret of being happy at any time in everything that happens, when I have enough to eat and when I go hungry, when I have more than I need and when I do not have enough. I can do all things through

Christ, because he gives me strength."
—the Apostle Paul, from Philippians 4:12b-13

discussion questions

- What do you think it means to "fall in love with your problems"?
- How can we avoid falling in love with our problems?
- Is it possible to avoid all disappointment? Why or why not?
- Have you ever set yourself up to be disappointed? Explain.
- What is Paul's secret to being content in all situations?
- Do you think Paul was ever disappointed? If so, how do you think he dealt with it? If not, what did he know that you and I don't?

Say: **Our perspective has a lot to do with how we handle disappointment. If we focus on what goes wrong in our lives, we can become very discouraged when we face disappointment. If we focus on God and realize that God brings good out of suffering, like Paul, we can be content in every situation.**

☞**Reality Bites**

TOPIC: Discouragement
THE POINT: Sin poisoned the world.
SCRIPTURE: Deuteronomy 30:19-20
TIME: 5 to 10 minutes

Form pairs so kids can discuss their reactions to one or both of these quotes:

"You look around you, you see nothing real. But at least pain is real."

—Hard Harry in the movie *Pump Up the Volume*
(*13th Gen* by Neil Howe and Bill Strauss)

"The way society presents it, I'll either be strung out on drugs, a manager at McDonald's, or a lawyer."

—Jill Nelson, high school student, Washington D.C.

(*13th Gen* by Neil Howe and Bill Strauss)

discussion questions

- Are you hopeful about your future? Why or why not?
- Who's fault is it that the world isn't perfect?
- Since God allowed Adam and Eve to sin in the first place, isn't it his fault that we get disappointed in life? Why or why not?

Have a volunteer read Deuteronomy 30:19-20 aloud. Ask:

- Who chose sin in the first place?
- Have you ever chosen sin over life? Why or why not?
- Whose fault is it that we get disappointed and discouraged? Explain.

Say: **God didn't cause sin. He gave us the freedom to make our own choices. That freedom extends to choosing whether we live in close relationship with God or choosing to let sin separate us from him. Because humanity chose to sin, the world is poisoned. That's why we all get discouraged and disappointed.**

☞ Personal Power

TOPIC: God's Word

THE POINT: God's Word has the power to change you.

TIME: 5 to 10 minutes

Form pairs, and give each pair paper and a pencil. Say: **With your partner, find as many mirrorlike objects in this room as you can. For example, you might be able to see your reflection in a doorknob or a window. You have three minutes to find the objects and write down what they are. Ready? Set? Go!**

After three minutes, determine which pair found the most mirrorlike objects and what those objects were. Then have kids discuss these questions in their pairs:

discussion questions

● If you wanted to see whether you need to change something about your appearance, which of the mirrorlike objects in this room would you look into? Why?

● How is reading the Bible like looking into some of these objects? How is it different?

● Where do you look to find out what you need to change inside yourself?

● How does God's Word have the power to change you?

● Will this activity change how often you look into your Bible? Why or why not?

☞Peace vs. Pain

TOPIC: Life Struggles

THE POINT: Suffering is a normal part of life.

TIME: 10 to 15 minutes

Have kids form two groups. Instruct each group to choose one person to be a Nerve Ending and another person to be a Pain Prompter.

Say: **Both groups will compete against each other in a race around the church building** (or, if more appropriate, around your meeting room). **During the race you must** protect your Nerve Endings from any "pain" they may experience. In this game, pain can be any feeling of unpleasantness. For example, someone may bump into your Nerve Ending as you run the race or your Nerve Ending may feel upset about a piece of trash on the ground. As a group, surround your Nerve Ending to protect him or her from pain.

But while you're trying to protect your Nerve Ending, the other group's Pain Prompter will try to cause him or her "pain." We're *not* talking about inflicting real pain such as hitting, kicking, or *anything* violent. Instead, Pain Prompters will do harmless things that might annoy or bother the Nerve Endings, such as talking loudly to the Nerve Endings or throwing paper wads at them.

At the end of the race, the Nerve Endings will report the "kinds of pain" they felt—the group that best protects its Nerve Ending from pain will win. Ready? Go!

If you have a group of four or fewer kids, have kids form one group and race against the clock. Have one person volunteer to be the Pain Prompter.

After the race, have kids form foursomes to discuss these questions:

discussion questions

● Was protecting your Nerve Ending a difficult task? If so, why?

● How was trying to protect your Nerve Ending like trying to protect yourself from pain?

● Why is it so tough to completely isolate ourselves from hurt?

● What might be some advantages in avoiding suffering as a normal part of life? disadvantages?

● How might this activity change what you think about pain? how you respond to pain?

☞Never Alone

> **TOPIC:** Loneliness
> **THE POINT:** God is with you and wants to know you.
> **TIME:** 5 to 10 minutes

Give each student paper and a pencil. Say: **Write one fact that no one else in this room knows about you. Make sure it's something you don't mind others knowing. For example, you could write, "I once had ten stitches in my chin."**

When everyone has finished, collect and shuffle the papers. Have students sit in a circle and each take a paper, preferably not his or her own. Say: **Now let's play a game. Each of you will read aloud the paper you now hold. Then everyone will try to guess who wrote it.** Go around the circle until the group identifies who wrote each statement. Have kids form pairs and discuss the following questions.

discussion questions

- What was difficult about this game?
- How did you feel when others figured out which statement you wrote?
- Does this game change how you feel about others in the room? Why or why not?
- How is this activity like the way God knows you? How is it different?
- Do you think God is with you and wants to know you? Why or why not?
- How does it affect you to realize that God knows everything about you?
- Why is it important to God to know you so well?

☞ Power Within

> **TOPIC:** The Occult
> **THE POINT:** Satan isn't equal to God in power or authority.
> **TIME:** 5 to 10 minutes

Read to your kids this true story about a sixteen-year-old girl:

Sometimes the dark scares Linda.* Sometimes menacing voices inside her head dictate pages of mysterious messages to her. Sometimes her eyes appear icy cold. Sometimes she thinks of suicide.

Linda went to church most of her life. But one day at a party, her friends invited her to experiment with a Ouija board. This seemingly innocent toy-store game created an unquenchable thirst within Linda to gain more power. She eventually became involved in astrology, tarot cards, witchcraft, and voodoo magic.

But now the voices in her head, voices that had once comforted her and given her powerful knowledge, haunt her. As many as seven distinct demonic spirits control Linda, manipulating her like a puppet.

Linda wants out, but the power she once craved has made her its slave.

(*Not her real name)

After the story, have students form trios to discuss the following questions.

discussion questions

- What's your reaction to this story?
- How does the statement "Satan isn't equal to God in power or authority" affect your feelings about this story?
- What would you say to Linda if you met her? Why?
- Is playing with a Ouija board, reading tarot cards, or following a horoscope

wrong? Why or why not?
- Do you believe the devil and demons exist? Why or why not?
- What kind of power do you want? How can you get it?

☞ Always Accepted

TOPIC: Popularity
THE POINT: God's treasure is in you.
TIME: 5 to 10 minutes

Form pairs so kids can discuss their reactions to one or both of these quotes:

"I remember a girl I knew in high school who always seemed to be happy. She sure didn't appear to worry much about doing things right. She was fun, popular, and the life of the party. She was also incredibly beautiful and never without a date. At my ten-year high school reunion, I honestly didn't recognize her. After two failed marriages and a couple of abortions, her 'fun' had caught up with her."

—Jim Burns, president of the National Institute of Youth Ministries

("Let's Talk," 1995 Christianity Today, Inc./Campus Life magazine, from America Online)

"Jennifer often dreams of trying out for the cheerleading squad. But Jennifer's not really interested in cheerleading. She's interested in popularity. So Jennifer, like so many middle schoolers struggling with their self-esteem,

pays more attention to the cheerleading clique than the other cliques."
—Jolene L. Roehlkepartain, author
("Why Kids Clique," Jr. High Ministry magazine, April/May 1992)

discussion questions

- What's your reaction to these quotes?
- What's your opinion of Jennifer? of the person Jim Burns described?
- How have these people treated God's treasure in them?
- What do these quotes tell you about pursuing popularity?
- How do these quotes affect whether you'll protect God's treasure in you?
- Have you been seeking to become a popular person? Explain.
- Have you been protecting God's treasure in you? Explain.

☞More Than Words

> TOPIC: Prayer
> THE POINT: God always answers your prayers.
> TIME: 5 to 10 minutes

Form pairs so kids can discuss their reactions to one or more of these discussion starters. If time allows, have pairs report the results of their discussion to the rest of the class.

discussion questions

- Finish this sentence: "If my prayers were jewelry, they'd be..." (for example, "diamonds because they're precious to God" or "fake pearls—they look good on the outside but are cheap on the inside").

- Describe a time when you knew for sure that God answered one of your prayers.
- Describe a time when you prayed but nothing happened.
- Finish this sentence with at least three descriptive words: "My prayer life over the last thirty days has been..." Explain why you chose the words you did.
- When are you most likely to pray? Why? When are you most likely not to pray? Why?
- Do you think God *always* answers your prayers? Explain.
- Tell your partner what you'd say the biggest prayer need is in your life right now. Then take a moment to pray (either silently or aloud) for your partner.

☞ Too-Cool Kids

> **TOPIC:** Pride
> **THE POINT:** Pride stops the flow of forgiveness.
> **TIME:** 5 to 10 minutes

Form pairs so kids can discuss their reactions to one or both of these quotes:

"Their casual acceptance of violence, the attitude...that any means is OK to get what you want, and the fatalism that kills their hope of the future is turning them into a generation of animals."

—William Raspberry, in an article about teenagers (Washington Post)

"I feel stupid and contagious."

—From the song "Smells Like Teen Spirit" by Nirvana

discussion questions

● What do you think of these quotes?

● Why are some people calling you "a generation of animals"?

● Do you feel "stupid and contagious"? Why or why not?

● How would you respond to William Raspberry or Kurt Cobain of Nirvana for making these comments?

● How do comments like these make you feel about your generation? yourself?

● Based on your reaction to these quotes, do you think pride can stop the flow of forgiveness? Why or why not?

☞ A Code to Live By

> TOPIC: Purpose
> THE POINT: God wants you to have integrity.
> TIME: 10 to 15 minutes

Say: **We're going to play a game that actors play to learn how to work together. One person begins by making a motion and an accompanying sound. Then another person interacts with the first by making a new motion and a different sound.**

For example, one of you could stand up straight, clasp your hands, swing your arms from side to side, and say "ticktock" again and again. Then another one of you could get on your knees in front of the first person, swing your arms in the same manner, and say "whoosh" each

time you swing your arms. Another one of you could stand behind the first person, swing your arms over the first person's head, and say "bop" each time you do so.

All of you will join in until everyone is part of a "machine." You don't have to touch each other, but you do need to interact with at least one of the other "machine parts."

Let students begin the game. Once everyone is participating, let the machine "run" for fifteen seconds. Then have students form trios to discuss these questions:

discussion questions

- Once the machine was running, was it easy or hard to keep it going? Explain.
- What would have happened if one of you had stopped or decided to go in a different direction?
- How did keeping your actions consistent help the whole machine work?
- How is keeping your actions consistent in this game like keeping your actions consistent with your beliefs? How is it different? Explain.
- Have you ever said one thing and then done another? If so, how did you feel? How did others react?
- Do you think God ever says one thing and then does another? Why or why not?
- Do you think God wants you to have integrity? Why or why not?

☞ The Absolute Truth

TOPIC: Right and Wrong
THE POINT: God's holiness sets the standard for right and wrong.
TIME: 5 to 10 minutes

Form trios so kids can discuss their reactions to these quotes:

"There is no such thing as an absolute, objective point of view in matters of morality and religion. A common expression of this assumption is the statement 'You have your truth and I have mine.'"

"Subjective experience supersedes logic and objective facts. We are free to choose what we will believe according to what makes us feel comfortable. Don't confuse us with the facts."

"The nature of truth and the nature of God are relative, not absolute, concepts: 'You have your god and I have mine.'"

(Source: *Jesus for a New Generation* by Kevin Graham Ford)

discussion questions

● What's your reaction to the first quote? the second? the third?

● Which quote do you agree with most? Explain.

● Which quote do you disagree with most? Explain.

● Do you think your beliefs about these quotes are typical of most kids your age? Why or why not?

● If a friend of yours told you he or she believed everything these quotes say, how would you respond?

● Can a person believe these statements and also believe that God's holiness sets the standard for right and wrong? Why or why not?

● Do you believe that God's holiness sets the standard for right and wrong? Why or why not?

☞Voice Mail

> **TOPIC:** Salvation
> **THE POINT:** The Spirit of Christ lives in you.
> **TIME:** 10 to 15 minutes

Recruit an adult leader or a student to help you. Privately direct your volunteer to give a series of instructions to the group. For example, the volunteer may tell group members to touch their toes, jump in place, and put their hands on their heads. Tell your volunteer to keep giving instructions until you signal to stop.

Have students stand in a group with their backs to you and the volunteer. Say: (Volunteer's name) **will give you some instructions to follow. Your task is to do whatever** (volunteer's name) **tells you to do.** Have the volunteer begin to give instructions. As he or she does so, yell different instructions. For example, tell kids to put their fingers in their ears, cover their eyes, and skip around the room. Make sure your voice is louder than your volunteer's.

After one minute, have kids form trios to discuss the following questions.

discussion questions

- What were you thinking and feeling as you tried to follow (volunteer's) instructions?
- How was trying to follow (volunteer's) instructions like trying to listen to the Holy Spirit, the Spirit of Christ living in you, when other religions compete for your attention? How was it different?
- What are some ways the Holy Spirit might communicate with you?
- What are some things that you can do to hear the Holy Spirit in the midst of other voices?
- Have you ever heard and followed the Holy Spirit before? If so, what happened? If not, why do you think you haven't heard and/or followed him?

● What's one thing you can do this week to be better in touch with the Holy Spirit?

☞Free to Be Me

TOPIC: Self-Image
THE POINT: Only Jesus can free you to be yourself.
TIME: 10 to 15 minutes

Hand each student a sheet of paper and a pen. Say: **We're going to play an old game with a new twist. On your paper, write two truths and one lie about yourself. The two truths should be things you've discovered about yourself through others, such as your family, friends, or God. For example, a friend might have told you that you're good at keeping secrets. The lie should be something someone said about you that's not true. For example, a teacher may have said that you're a forgetful person, but you know you're not.**

Don't write your statements in any particular order. You'll read all three of your statements to the group, and the group will try to guess which statement is the lie.

When everyone has written two truths and a lie, have each person read his or her statements to the group, and have the group vote on which statement is the lie. Then have the student reveal the correct answer.

After everyone has had a turn, have kids form trios to discuss these questions:

discussion questions

● Which was harder for you to think of—the truths or the lie? Explain.
● Which has had a greater impact on how you view yourself—the truths or the lie? Explain.
● What were you thinking or feeling as you revealed parts of your identity to the group?

- What's the best way to discover who you truly are?
- What's your reaction to the following statement: "Only Jesus can free you to be yourself"?
- How has God shown you truths about yourself?

☞Worth the Wait

> TOPIC: Sexual Abstinence
> THE POINT: Sex creates a bond that thrives only in marriage.
> TIME: 5 to 10 minutes

Have students form trios and take turns reading aloud the following quotes to their groups. Then discuss the questions on page 57.

"Maybe I'm a little old-fashioned, but why people do something which could . . . lock you into something you don't want, or leave you with more responsibility than you might be able to handle is beyond me. Sex is natural, but without . . . placing moral restraints upon ourselves, we become the animals we pride ourselves on being superior to."
—Male, 18

"What can be wrong with having sex when you're fifteen if you truly care about the person, it's a wonderful experience for both of you, and you love each other before and after sex?"
—Female, 16

"Sex is sacred. It is of utmost importance to me, so that's why I'm still a virgin."

—Male, 17

(Source: *Ask Me if I Care* by Nancy Rubin)

discussion questions

● What's your reaction to these quotes?

● Do you think the teenagers who said these words are Christians? Why or why not?

● Should Christians view sex differently from non-Christians? Why or why not?

● If you were asked to add you own words about sex to these quotes, what would be the most important thing you could say?

● Why would God tell these young people not to have sex before marriage?

● The Bible teaches that sex creates a bond that thrives only in marriage. Do you think that's true? Why or why not?

☞Adrenalin Junkies

> **TOPIC:** Teenage Thrill Seekers
> **THE POINT:** The Holy Spirit empowers you to live life's greatest adventures.
> **TIME:** 10 to 15 minutes

Say: **Let's evaluate our own cravings for thrill and adventure.**

Have students work together to choose four physical poses, each of which represents one of the following four attitudes:

Attitude 1: Has no interest at all in thrills or adventures.

Attitude 2: Likes to watch or hear about adventures but is not interested in actually having an adrenalin rush.

Attitude 3: Helps others in their adventures (such as

handling the ropes while another person rappels).

Attitude 4: Seeks thrills and makes adventures happen.

When the four positions have been determined, have each person assume the position that best describes him or her. Then have kids each find a partner who has a different attitude toward adventure from their own. (It's OK if some students have to pair up with a like-minded person.) Ask kids to discuss the following questions with their partners.

discussion questions

● What's an example from your life that explains why you chose the position you did?

● Why do you think some people crave an adrenalin rush?

● What would be your ultimate rush or thrill?

● Is there a difference between an adrenalin rush and a real adventure? Why or why not?

● What would be your ultimate adventure?

● How is following the Holy Spirit like an adventure?

● What's your reaction to this statement: "The Holy Spirit empowers you to live life's greatest adventures"? Explain.

● What adventures do you think the Holy Spirit might lead you to this year?

☞Just Say Know

TOPIC: Teen Experimentation

THE POINT: Satan has a plan for your life.

TIME: 5 to 10 minutes

Have kids form pairs to discuss their reactions to these quotes:

"For [teenage compulsive gamblers], the adrenalin rush of betting is priority No. 1. It ranks above school or friends or growing debt; it can drive

them to steal or sell drugs for betting cash; it can hound them to suicide."
—(J. Taylor Buckley, "Nation raising 'a generation of gamblers,' "
USA Today, April 5, 1995)

"There's no doubt in my mind
that cigarettes are a gateway drug. About
five months after I started smoking I
started doing drugs. I'm in Narcotics
Anonymous for marijuana and alcohol abuse.
Almost everyone I know, except for three
people, started smoking BEFORE doing
drugs. That has to tell you something."
—Sabrina Hall, age 13
(Newsweek magazine)

*"When Satan comes he never
comes dragging the chains that will
confine us. He comes bringing a crown
that will ennoble us. He comes offering
us pleasure, expansiveness, money,
popularity, freedom, enjoyment. In fact,
he never really says there are any con-
sequences at all, just that we will fill all
the desires of our hearts. It is there we
are destroyed."*
—("Sermon: Don't Doubt God's Goodness" by Haddon W. Robinson,
Christianity Today, Inc./Leadership Journal, 1995, from America Online)

discussion questions
- According to these quotes, how do small
  temptations lead to the fulfillment of
  Satan's plan for your life?
- How does Satan's plan unfold?
- What temptation that you're facing might
  turn into a bigger problem? into the ful-
  fillment of Satan's plan for your life?
- How can you respond to that temptation so
  you can avoid Satan's plan for you?

◄Reaching Out

REACHING   OUT   REACHING   OUT

REACHING   OUT   REACHING   OUT

REACHING   OUT   REACHING   OUT

REACHING   OUT   REACHING   OUT

REACHING   OUT   REACHING   OUT

REACHING   OUT   REACHING   OUT

REACHING   OUT   REACHING   OUT

REACHING   OUT   REACHING   OUT

☞Rock-a-Bye Baby

> **TOPIC:** Abortion
> **THE POINT:** Your family is important to God.
> **TIME:** 5 to 10 minutes

Have kids form pairs to discuss their reactions to these quotes:

"I was pregnant at fifteen, and I decided to have an abortion. It was the best way to deal with it, in my opinion."

"I got pregnant at fifteen and had an abortion. It was the hardest and most painful thing I have ever done. To this day two years later it still makes me cry."

"Once I decided to keep [the baby] my mother and father had different responses. My mother was 100 percent supportive, my father was about 90 percent because he thought the baby was going to hold me back from my dreams. But now they are both more excited than I sometimes am. They walk around telling folks that they are going to be grandparents."

"My mom works for an adoption agency, and a lot of these kids have a much better life after they were adopted. Not to say that anyone couldn't take care of their child, but with adoption you could give your child things that you couldn't if you had kept him/her... It's much better than abortion, in my opinion."

"I'm fourteen and I'm pregnant, but not by choice. I was raped and this is a result. I have no idea what I'm going to do ... I don't know whether to keep the baby or abort it. I just know I'm scared, confused, and in trouble."

(Source: an America Online message board on teen pregnancy)

discussion questions

● What's your reaction to these quotes?
● How do you think God feels about these quotes? about these kids?
● Which of these people do you most agree with? disagree with? Explain.
● Which of these quotes best reflects the idea that your family is important to God? Why?
● If you could tell any one (or all) of these girls anything about abortion, what would you tell them? Why?
● If you could tell any one (or all) of these girls anything about how God values the family, what would you tell them? Why?

☞Cry Freedom

TOPIC: Abuse

THE POINT: God allows everyone the freedom to choose.

TIME: 5 to 10 minutes

Form pairs so kids can discuss their reactions to these situations:

1. Craig Rogers filed a $2.5 million sexual-harassment suit against a

California State University lesbian psychology professor. Rogers, an evangelical Christian student, claimed that anti-male bias in one of her lectures violated campus rules and left him feeling "raped and trapped."

2. At the University of Michigan, a student involved in a classroom discussion said that he considered homosexuality a disease treatable with therapy. He was summoned to a formal disciplinary hearing for violating the school's policy against speech that "victimizes" people based on "sexual orientation."

3. A Pennsylvania court found that an employer's decision to print Bible verses on paychecks constituted religious harassment of Jewish employees.

(Source: Jonathan Rauch, "In Defense of Prejudice," Harper's Magazine, May 1995)

discussion questions

- Was there abuse in any of these situations? Why or why not?
- What are some examples of abuse you wish God would prevent?
- Why doesn't God stop abuse?
- How does the fact that God allows everyone freedom to make his or her own choices explain why God allows abuse to happen?
- Why do you think people choose to abuse each other?
- What do you think is the best way to respond in a physically abusive situation?

☞ Untouchables

> **TOPIC:** AIDS
> **THE POINT:** Love is a choice that leads to action.
> **SCRIPTURE:** Psalm 103:1-10
> **TIME:** 5 to 10 minutes

Have kids form foursomes and discuss their reactions to these quotations:

> "Many people have called me a hero because I've chosen to dedicate the rest of my life to educating people—especially teenagers—about HIV and how to protect themselves from it. But let me be clear about one thing: I'm not a hero because I got HIV. And I didn't get HIV because I was a 'bad' person or a 'dirty' one or someone who 'deserved' it for whatever reason. No one 'deserves' to get HIV. I got HIV because I had unprotected sex. I got HIV because I thought HIV could never happen to someone like me."

—"Magic" Johnson

(*My Life* by Earvin "Magic" Johnson with William Novak)

> "When he stood on the podium to receive his second medal [at the 1988 Olympics], Louganis recalls wondering, 'How soon before I get sick?...What would the people cheering for me think if they knew I was gay and HIV-positive? Would they still cheer?'"

—Greg Louganis

(Time magazine, excerpted from his autobiography, *Breaking the Surface*)

discussion questions

● What's your reaction to these quotations?

- Did your impressions of these athletes change when you found out they were HIV-positive? Explain.
- How do you feel about interacting with people who have HIV or AIDS?
- Read Psalm 103:1-10. How can these verses apply to people who have HIV or AIDS?
- Why do you think God allows people to get AIDS?
- How can you show love to people such as Magic Johnson and Greg Louganis? to others you know who have HIV or AIDS?

☞Cult Repellent

> **TOPIC:** Cults
> **THE POINT:** Faith in Jesus is the only way to eternal life.
> **TIME:** 5 to 10 minutes

Give everyone paper and a pencil. Say: **I'm going to ask you seven questions about your spiritual commitment. On your paper, answer "yes" or "no" to each question. Would you be willing to...**
- **leave your family if a spiritual leader told you to?**
- **hand over control of your money to a church leader?**
- **put yourself under the authority of a spiritual leader?**
- **accept your church's teachings without question?**
- **allow a spiritual leader to tell you who to marry?**
- **separate yourself from everyone who does not belong to your church?**
- **let a spiritual leader tell you what the Bible means?**

Have kids give themselves one point for each "yes" answer. Then say: **Spiritual commitment can be good, but it's disastrous to give up control of our lives to anyone other than Jesus. Unfortunately, cult leaders often use our desire to live for God to lure us into their cults. So the**

higher you scored on this test, the greater the danger that you'll fall under the influence of a cult. Divide kids into three or four groups, and have them discuss the following questions.

discussion questions

● How can God use your desire for spiritual commitment?
● How can a cult exploit your desire for spiritual commitment?
● How can you avoid committing yourself to the wrong person or organization?
● How can knowing that Jesus is the way to eternal life help you avoid cults?

☞Love Struck

> **TOPIC:** Dating
> **THE POINT:** Relationships take work and commitment.
> **TIME:** 10 to 15 minutes

Photocopy one "On Dating and Marriage" handout (p. 68) for each student in your class. Have kids form pairs so they can discuss their reactions to these ideas. Provide each pair with pencil and paper.

discussion questions

● List on your paper advantages and disadvantages to the dating system in our society.
● What are the advantages and disadvantages to the betrothal system? List these also.
● If you created a new way of courting that took the best of both the dating and betrothal systems, what would it look like?
● Does your system support the belief that relationships take work and commitment? Why or why not?

On **Dating** And Marriage

Arranged Marriages Back In Vogue?

What's your reaction to this statement?

"The Bible doesn't endorse dating; in fact, arranged marriages are what God intended."

Sound a bit extreme? Well, an article supporting this belief appeared in Patriarch, a Christian men's magazine. Among other things, the article stated:

● Dating is a temporary romantic relationship that's designed to eventually end. Thus it teaches us more about divorce than it does about marriage.

● When the Bible says to love your husband or wife, that means to love the one you are married to. It doesn't mean to marry the one you love.

● Dating encourages people to form emotional bonds without permanent commitment. That means you become emotionally close to someone without the security of knowing he or she will be in this relationship with you permanently.

The Betrothal System

Mary and Joseph weren't just "engaged" in the sense we know it today— they were "betrothed" to each other.
What's the difference?

During Mary and Joseph's time, Hebrew families typically arranged their children's marriages. This arrangement was sealed with a legally binding contract between the families involved. Once the children reached their early teenage years, they were officially "betrothed." From then on they were considered married and were called husband and wife, even though each person continued to live with his or her own family. This living situation continued for one year to prove the sexual purity of the bride. (In other words, if she became pregnant during this time, she obviously wasn't sexually pure.) After a year, the husband would go to his wife's home and claim his bride. They would then live together and physically consummate their marriage.

When Luke refers to Mary and Joseph's engagement, he is saying the couple was in this one-year betrothal period. When Mary became pregnant, Joseph could've legally divorced her. However, he took her into his home earlier than the custom allowed, but did not consummate their marriage physically until after the year was up. It's likely that Joseph's decision evoked a great deal of gossip and ridicule from the townsfolk, but Mary and Joseph both knew the truth and chose to withstand the pressures of their culture.

☞When the Vow Breaks

TOPIC: Divorce
THE POINT: God's love never fails you.
SCRIPTURE: Psalm 31:1-2, 21-22
TIME: 10 to 15 minutes

Form groups of four. **Say: As a group, you have three minutes to build a fort. You may build it out of anything you can find—books, furniture, whatever. Go!**

After three minutes, call time and admire the forts. Have foursomes discuss these questions:

● **How secure do you think you would be inside your fort?**
● **In what ways can a secure family or home life be like a fort for you?**

Then say: **Let's see how structurally sound these forts really are. When I point to your fort, pull out one object that is part of the fort. The object you choose must be touching the floor.**

One by one, have groups remove an object from their forts. Continue having groups remove one object at a time until every fort has collapsed. Then have groups discuss the following questions.

discussion questions

● How is what happened to your fort like what happens to a family when parents divorce?
● How would you (or did you) feel about your parents divorcing?

Have groups read Psalm 31:1-2, 21-22 and then discuss:

● How can God be like a secure fort for you when everything seems to be falling apart?
● When have you felt that security in God?
● How can you trust that God's love never fails you? Explain.

☞**Intensive Care**

TOPIC: Family

THE POINT: God can heal your family's hurts.

SCRIPTURE: Genesis 37:18-28; 45:1-15

TIME: 10 to 15 minutes

Say: **Family relationships have always been difficult. Even people in the Bible experienced hardships with parents and siblings. Let's explore this a little more.**

Enlist volunteers to play the parts of Joseph, Reuben, Judah, and a Midianite trader. If you want to involve the entire class, have up to eight play the parts of Joseph's other brothers, and have the rest play the parts of the other Midianite traders.

Say: **I'm going to read aloud the story of Joseph and his brothers. If you hear me read something about your character, mime whatever actions fit the story. Remember to be careful as you interact with other characters.** Then read Genesis 37:18-28 aloud, pausing as necessary to allow kids to act out their parts.

When the group has finished the "play," have students form pairs to discuss these questions:

discussion questions

● Who suffered in this story? Why?
● How is Joseph's family like your family? How is it different?
● Is anyone in your family experiencing hurt as a result of relationships within the family? If so, who and why?
● Read Genesis 45:1-15. How did God heal family hurts in Joseph's story?
● How might God heal your family's hurts? How might God use you to accomplish this?

☞ Cyberfriends

TOPIC: Friendship

THE POINT: You need real-life relationships in the church.

TIME: 10 to 15 minutes

Have kids form groups of four. Have each group member take one of the following roles: Communicator 1, Communicator 2, Computer 1, or Computer 2. Then have each foursome form a line according to these instructions: Communicator 1 faces Computer 1, Computer 2 stands with his or her back to Computer 1, and Communicator 2 stands facing Computer 2.

Say: **Communicators 1 and 2, your task is to have a conversation with each other. Discuss what you like and dislike about online relationships. However, you may not speak to each other directly. Instead, you must communicate through the Computers facing you. Whisper to your Computer what you'd like to tell the other Communicator in your group. Computers, when you hear a message from your Communicator, whisper the message to the other Computer. When you hear a message from the other Computer, relay that message to your Communicator.**

When everyone understands the activity, let groups begin. After three minutes, have foursomes discuss the following questions.

discussion questions

● Communicators, how was communicating through your computers like communicating with others online? How was it different?

● Computers, what were you thinking and feeling as you communicated messages back and forth?

● How did communicating in this way affect how you related to the others in your group?

● Do you agree or disagree with the following statement: "You need real-life relationships in the church"? Explain.

● What's one thing you can do this week to cultivate a real-life relationship?

☞Forgive Me

> **TOPIC:** Friendship
> **THE POINT:** Sin can destroy your relationships.
> **TIME:** 10 to 15 minutes

Have kids form pairs so they can discuss their reactions to this story. If you have a dramatically inclined young person, consider asking him or her to read the story aloud—otherwise, read the story yourself.

They killed him in the most horrible way known in those days. They nailed him to wooden beams, and dangled him—hung him—above the ground. The muscles in his arms and legs tore a little each time he tried to pull himself up so he could breathe. They condemned him to a slow, slow death. Sometimes criminals would hang there alive for days. As if that weren't enough, they watched, relishing his pain, taunting him, jeering at him.

"Hey, mister, if you're so great, how come you can't save yourself?"

"Prophet? Healer? Deliverer? He's nothing."

"I thought you said you were God. Well, we killed you, God. We killed you!"

His trial had been a joke. Instead of being questioned, he was taunted and tortured. They traded his life for a man who had committed murder. Not even the top government officials would come down on the side of justice. And just a day later, they crucified him. They even gambled for his clothes—the only possessions he had left.

His response? "Father, forgive them. They don't know what they're doing."

And so he was God. Only God could have responded with such absolute love.

discussion questions

● What's your response to this story?
● If one of your friends were killed in such a horrible way, could you forgive those responsible? Why or why not?

- If you had been present at the Crucifixion, what would you have said to Jesus? Explain.
- What do you think he would've said to you?
- What does this story tell you about forgiveness? about Jesus? about your relationships?
- How can sin destroy your relationships?

☞Stand by Me

> **TOPIC:** Gangs
>
> **THE POINT:** True friends inspire excellence.
>
> **TIME:** 10 to 15 minutes

Photocopy and enlarge the quotes from the "Gang Talk" box (p. 74), then cut apart and tape the quotes in different places around the room.

Have kids read the quotes you've posted, and say: **Stand by the quote that sounds the *least* like friendship to you.** When kids have chosen a quote, have them pair up with someone standing near them. Have pairs discuss their answers to the following questions.

discussion questions

- Why did you choose the quote you're standing by?
- What does that quote tell you about friendship?
- Are there times when you're a friend like that? Explain.

After kids have discussed those questions, say: **Stand by the quote that sounds the most like friendship to you.** When kids have chosen quotes, have them pair up with someone new. Have pairs answer the same questions above for the quotes they chose. Then ask:

- What have you learned about friendship from these quotes?
- How will you change the way you're a friend based on this activity?

Gang Talk

"The term 'wilding' refers to young people cruising in a pack, roaming the streets, and violently attacking passersby for 'fun.'"
—(*Street Gangs in America* by Sandra Gardner)

"To join the Play Girl Gangsters, Regina had to fight two gang members at once for a count of 60, ending up bloodied and bruised. In return, she got a new gang name, a tattoo, and a group of 20 or 30 girls willing, in theory at least, to kill and die for her."
—(Gini Sikes, "Girls in the Hood," Scholastic Update, February 11, 1994)

"He's this small little punk but wants a name, right? So you make him do the work. 'Hey, homey, get me a car. A red car. A red sports car. By tonight. I'm taking my woman out. Or hey, homey, go find me $50. Or hey, little homey, you wanna be big? Go pop that nigger that's messing with our business.'"
—Keith, 17, gang member (Time magazine, September 19, 1994)

"A lot of my homeboys and homegirls are homeless...Their mothers can't afford them, so they send them out on the street. We have barbecues and picnics for the kids who don't have homes. No one ever writes about that."
—Regina, nineteen, gang member (Gini Sikes, "Girls in the Hood," Scholastic Update, February 11, 1994)

"Nicole had recently lost her father... Now she had turned to Nick [and had sex with him]. I knew I wasn't being a true friend if I didn't remind her what Jesus would think. But I was scared. I knew I was risking a lot. She could either be thankful that I reminded her, and try to turn herself around, or she could get mad—and I would lose her friendship. But I had to take that risk. I couldn't be selfish about a friendship...

"Sometimes friendship is risky business. But knowing that Jesus risked everything to come to earth and die on a wooden cross makes it easy to take that risk for someone you call a friend."
—Beth, Christian teenager (*Over the Edge and Back* by Joe White)

"We can't sugar-coat stuff....Jesus got beat down. People need to know what He went through for us...He did it willingly, knowing what He was doing because He loves all of us."
—Dove, member of Gospel Gangstas, a Christian rap group (Contemporary Christian Music, October, 1994)

☞At What Cost?

> TOPIC: Gentleness
> THE POINT: God's Spirit gives you strength to be gentle.
> TIME: 5 to 10 minutes

Form pairs so kids can discuss their reactions to one or both of the following quotes.

"Dan had been bullying another boy, Peter, since the beginning of the year. It started when he stole Peter's hat... [The assistant principal] thought it was resolved, but when Dan leaned forward to punch Peter that day, Peter thrust a knife into Dan's stomach."

—(Jan Johnson and Jim Burns, "When Violence Goes to School," Parents of Teenagers magazine, January/February 1995)

"According to the prosecution, Calvin Broadus and McKinley Lee hunted down rival gang member Philip Woldermariam and killed him. Broadus had moved into Woldermariam's neighborhood. Woldermariam went to his apartment and shouted insults. Broadus retaliated."

—(Susan Estrich, "New Lessons in Case of Snoop Doggy Dogg," USA Today, December 7, 1995)

discussion questions

- Do you agree with the reaction these people had to the insults they received? Why or why not?
- How do you feel after you've been insulted or bullied?
- Have you ever been "just joking" with someone and found out later that you really hurt his or her feelings? Explain.

- Has anyone ever hurt your feelings when he or she was just kidding with you? Why did you take the joking personally?
- Is it possible to know when joking has gone too far? If so, how?

Say: **God wants us to have fun and to laugh, but he doesn't want us to do it at the expense of others. It's important that we remain sensitive to the feelings of others as well as to God's direction. God's Spirit gives you strength to be gentle and sensitive to others.**

☞Hot Talk

TOPIC: Gossip

THE POINT: Your words reveal your character.

SCRIPTURE: Romans 1:28-32

TIME: 5 to 10 minutes

Pass out a pencil and slip of paper to everyone. Have the group choose one first name that doesn't belong to anyone in the group. Say: **Write down one positive comment about who you chose. For example, you might write, "(name) is very bright" or "(name) has a great smile." When you're finished writing, put your slip of paper in your pocket.**

When kids have finished, say: **In just a second, I'm going to ask you to wander around the room. As you wander, whisper your sentence to only one other person. If someone whispers a sentence to you, change one word in the sentence—except for the name—and then whisper the revised sentence to someone else. For example, "(name) is very bright" might become "(name) is very dull." Keep doing this until I tell you to stop. Ready? Start wandering.**

After a few minutes, have students sit in a circle. Go around the circle, and have students say the sentence they were about to revise and pass along. Ask kids if they can identify the sentences they originated. Then have them form trios to discuss these questions:

discussion questions

- What's your reaction to this experience? Would you have wanted to be (name)? Why or why not?
- How was this experience like gossip? How was it different?
- Is gossip abusive talk? Explain.
- What are other abusive ways we sometimes talk?
- Have you ever gossiped about someone else or been the subject of gossip? If so, what was the experience like? What were the results?
- Do you believe that your words reveal your character? Why or why not?
- Read Romans 1:28-32. What does this passage say about gossip and abusive talk?
- How can we keep ourselves from speaking abusively?

☞Straight From the Heart

TOPIC: Love

THE POINT: Real love is a free gift.

SCRIPTURE: 1 Corinthians 13:4-7

TIME: 5 to 10 minutes

Form pairs so kids can discuss their reactions to these statistics:

Each day in America—it happens!
- 2,795 unwed teenage girls become mothers.
- 1,106 teenage girls get abortions.

● 4,219 teenagers contract sexually transmitted diseases.
● 80 teenagers are raped.

After discussing the following questions, read aloud 1 Corinthians 13:4-7. Then have kids find partners and tell one way they'll love unselfishly this week.

discussion questions

● How do these statistics make you feel?
● What would you say to someone who told you these statistics are the result of two people loving each other?
● Do you think these statistics reflect love or selfishness? Explain.
● Is real love ever selfish? Why or why not?
● When have you chosen love over selfishness? selfishness over love?
● Because real love is a free gift that expects nothing in return, what motivates you to love someone?
● Why does God love us without conditions?

☞ Not-So-Perfect Examples

TOPIC: Mentors
THE POINT: No human authority is perfect.
TIME: 10 to 15 minutes

Form trios. Say: **Think for one minute—if you could share a pizza with any two historical characters, who would they be?** After kids decide, ask them to share their answers in their trios, including why they chose the people they did. Once kids have shared, ask trios to select three of the characters their group mentioned and portray them for another trio so that the other trio can guess the names of the characters. Be sure every trio gets to perform and every trio gets to guess.

When students have finished, say: **We didn't all pick the same pizza partners, did we? That's because we find different sorts of characters fun, interesting, or admirable.**
Have trios discuss these questions:

discussion questions

● Would you say the historical characters you selected are heroes? Why or why not?

● Would you say the people you selected are perfect? Why or why not?

● Do you think there's any such thing as a perfect human authority? Why or why not?

● If no human authority is perfect, why should you try to follow any authority figure?

● Do you like the idea of having a Christian mentor? Why or why not?

● What could a Christian mentor do for you?

● If you were a Christian mentor, what could you do for others?

● How can we work together to find Christian mentors for us?

● How can we work together to find people that we can mentor?

☞Mission Possible

TOPIC: Missions

THE POINT: Doing good things won't get you into heaven.

TIME: 10 to 15 minutes

Have kids form trios. Tell kids that they'll send their trio members on "missions" to other class members. Explain that each mission must meet the following guidelines:

● A mission must impact at least one other member of the class.

● A mission must include a word or action designed to encourage someone, such as a compliment or a back rub.
● A mission must include sharing an idea for reaching out to the local community.

Have each trio designate one member as a Sender and the other two as Missionaries. Then have Senders assign specific missions to their Missionaries, designating which class members the Missionaries should reach out to and what the Missionaries should say and do.

When Missionaries have returned to their trios, have each trio designate another member to be the Sender and repeat the process. After the second mission, have each trio choose a third Sender and repeat the process again.

After the last mission, have trios discuss the following questions.

discussion questions

● What were you thinking and feeling as you went on your missions? as people came to you on their missions?
● How was this experience like going on a mission? How was it different?
● Have you ever participated in a mission to a local community? If so, what did you do, and what was your reaction to it?
● Do you agree with this statement: "Doing good things won't get you into heaven"? Why or why not?
● How does participating in missions in this class, in our community, or in another country affect whether you'll get to heaven?
● Based on this activity, would you like to go on a mission? Why or why not?

☞Bridge the Gap

TOPIC: Parents

THE POINT: Your parents need your respect and love.

TIME: 5 to 10 minutes

Form pairs so kids can discuss their reactions to one or both of these quotes.

"The best thing about my parents is...they are incredibly generous and want the best for me."

discussion questions

● What's the best thing about your parents?
● Do you think your parents want the best for you? How can you tell?
● What happens when you don't agree with your parents about what's best for you?

"The worst thing about my parents is...they tend to underestimate people my age."

discussion questions

● What's the worst thing about your parents?
● Do you think your parents underestimate people your age? How can you tell?
● How might you underestimate your parents?

After the discussion, say: **Developing good relationships with parents requires mutual love and respect. Your parents are more likely to respect you if you respect them too. Your parents need your respect and love.**

☞**Deal With It!**

TOPIC: Parents
THE POINT: God never changes.
TIME: 5 to 10 minutes

Have kids brainstorm, making a list of their favorite famous people. If possible, tape a sheet of newsprint to a wall, and write the names of athletes, musicians, actors, and other public figures that kids mention. Then have kids form pairs to discuss these questions:

discussion questions

- What is it about these people that draws you to them?
- Which of these famous people would you like to have as a father? Why?
- Which of these famous people would you like to have as a mother? Why?
- What does it take to be a good parent or stepparent?
- Do good parents or stepparents ever change? Why or why not?
- Why do parents and stepparents change?
- Can changes in your parents and stepparents be good? bad? Explain.
- How does the fact that God never changes affect your reactions to changes in your relationships with your parents or stepparents?

☞Embraced By Hope

TOPIC: Poverty

THE POINT: You can bring hope to the hurting.

TIME: 10 to 15 minutes

Have students form a circle. Say: **We're going to work together to come up with a list of ways you can bring hope to the hurting. I'll start by suggesting one way to help bring hope—physical, emotional, spiritual, or otherwise—such as listening to a depressed friend. Then the person to my right will say a different way. Our goal is to go around the circle as many times as we can without repeating a previously mentioned way to help. Remember, we're working on this together, so if someone gets stumped, gently help that person with a suggestion or two.**

When everyone understands the activity, begin by stating one way to help hurting people, such as helping an illiterate adult learn to read. As the activity progresses and kids have difficulty coming up with new ways to help, don't let them give up. Encourage kids to help each other out. Challenge them to come up with at least fifteen ways to help hurting people.

When it seems that you've exhausted all the possibilities, have each student turn to a partner to discuss the following questions.

discussion questions

● What's your reaction to this activity? to helping each other come up with answers? to working together toward a goal?

● How was the way you helped each other like how you can bring hope to the hurting? How was it different?

● What types of things stop us from helping others? Why?

- How can we overcome these things so we can bring hope to the hurting?
- Of the ways we listed, what's one thing you could do in the coming week to bring hope to someone who feels hurt?

☞ The Color of Hate

> **TOPIC:** Racism
> **THE POINT:** God's justice never fails.
> **SCRIPTURE:** Galatians 3:26-29
> **TIME:** 5 to 10 minutes

Form pairs so kids can discuss their reactions to these quotes:

"I have a dream that one day this nation will rise up and live out the true meaning of its creed...that all men are created equal...I have a dream that my four little children will one day live in a nation where they will not be judged by the color of their skin but by the content of their character. I have a dream today. And if America is to be a great nation, this must become true."
—Dr. Martin Luther King Jr., 1963

"We wanted a country where nobody would bother us and where there would be no problems—where we could all be at peace."
—Debi*

"If I could just push a button that would make me love all races, I wouldn't do it."
—"Eva"*

"White power, it creates a family for you. It's nice."

—Tim*

*(Teenage members of the Fourth Reich Skins. Rolling Stone magazine, June 30, 1994)

"I don't think there's anything wrong with saying I hate them [white people]. They have caused me harm over and over, and I wish they were dead."

—Sharod Baker, Nation of Islam member

("Pride and Prejudice," Time magazine, February 28, 1994)

discussion questions

● Which of these quotes do you most closely identify with? Explain.

● How do the aims of Dr. King, the Fourth Reich members, and the Nation of Islam member differ?

● If you could, what would you say to Martin Luther King Jr.? to Debi, Eva, and Tim? to Sharod Baker?

● Read Galatians 3:26-29. How are the Fourth Reich members' and Sharod Baker's beliefs different from Paul's teachings in this passage?

● How is Dr. King's dream like Paul's teachings?

● How will Paul's teachings impact how you view and treat people of other races and ethnic groups?

● How will the truth that "God's justice never fails" affect how you view and treat people of other races and ethnic groups?

☞ Trust Me!

TOPIC: Relationships
THE POINT: God is love.
TIME: 15 to 20 minutes

Ask kids to join you in the center of the room, then form two groups. Tell kids the class has been transformed into a talk show. Have one group act as the audience and the other group as a panel of celebrities who have all experienced betrayal.

Tell each panelist to assume the identity of a real-life person and to do their best to come up with a real-life story of betrayal in that person's life. Tell each audience member to compile a list of tough questions to ask the panelists. For example, "Who betrayed you? What happened? How did you respond? What was the most painful part of this betrayal? How did it affect your relationship? Is there anyone you trust completely? Why or why not?"

Act as the talk show host and introduce each panel member, then let the audience members ask their questions to discover just how each panelist felt betrayed.

After the panelists have told their stories, have kids form pairs by combining one audience member with one panelist. Then have pairs discuss the following questions.

discussion questions

- What elements were in nearly every story of betrayal?
- Which story of betrayal was most like one you've experienced?
- Is there someone you trust completely, who would never betray you?
- How does the fact that God is love affect your attitude toward betrayal?

Mark 10:21-23
Matt 26:21
1 John 4:7-21

☞Pass It On

TOPIC: Sharing Faith

THE POINT: You have to know your story before you can share it with others.

TIME: 10 to 15 minutes

Say: **Let's play a storytelling game—with a grand prize! The goal of the game is to tell the best real-life story you can—and we'll all vote on the winner. The winner will receive a fantastic prize. Your story can be funny, serious, or somewhere in between. Here are some questions to get you thinking:**

- **What's a story your parents tell about themselves or about you that people love to hear?**
- **What's a story about yourself that you love to tell?**

Give kids a few minutes to think, then ask for volunteers to come to the front and tell their stories. After you've had at least three storytellers (or more, if you'd like), ask for a volunteer to come to the front and serve as a human applause meter. Have your volunteer use his or her arm as a "needle" that goes up as the applause gets stronger. Then start the judging! Ask group members to vote on each person's story with their applause. The story that gets the most applause wins. (After the meeting, arrange to give the grand-prize winner a youth Bible or a CD by a Christian artist whose songs tell stories—such as Rich Mullins, Margaret Becker, or Sixpence None the Richer.)

After the contest, ask kids to form trios and discuss these questions:

discussion questions

- Why are family stories so important to us?
- Has your family's story been influenced by God? Why or why not?
- If you didn't know God, how would your own story be different right now?
- Why is it important to know your story and share it with others?
- How do you want others to be impacted by your story?

Handwritten margin notes:
Job 36:13-15.
1 Cor. 1:3-4, 6:7
friends comfort
Job 2:11
Job 119:49-52
Psalm

Why or what would cause someone to com. suicide?

☞On the Edge

TOPIC: Suicide

THE POINT: Forgiveness brings hope to life.

TIME: 5 to 10 minutes

Form pairs so kids can discuss their reactions to one or both of these quotes:

"Never, if I'd had a conscious thought of the intensity of the pain that has been caused, would I ever have had this happen. If I could do it all over. . . I would get help, seek help, cry out for and demand help, even more than I already did."

—Linda Christiansen, saying what she believes her son, Craig (a suicide victim), would say now if he were still alive.

"I realize that Kurt Cobain had a few more problems than we might, but him doing this, it kind of cheated us in a way. We figured if someone like him could make it out of a place like this...It was like he might have paved the way for the rest of us."

—Brandon Baker, a fifteen-year-old from Aberdeen, Washington (Cobain's hometown), commenting on Cobain's suicide.

discussion questions

● What's your reaction to these quotes?

● If you could've talked with Kurt or Craig one week before their deaths, what would you have said?

● What do you think was missing in Kurt Cobain's life?

● Do you think God can provide any real, immediate answers for kids who are considering suicide? Why or why not?

Encourage students to use indv. to locate verses on suffering, comfort, friendship.

- What do you think God would've wanted Kurt or Craig to know before they killed themselves?
- How does God's forgiveness bring hope to life?

☞Hear Me Out

> **TOPIC:** Teenage Runaways
> **THE POINT:** God is always ready to listen.
> **TIME:** 10 to 15 minutes

Hand out paper and pencils. Say: **You have sixty seconds to sketch pictures of items that would make your bedroom the perfect refuge or getaway—for example, your own phone, a favorite book to read, a particular snack, whatever. Use a separate sheet of paper for each item you draw. Go!**

After one minute, have kids arrange their pictures around themselves then find a partner. Have partners give each other "tours" of their ideal rooms.

Say: **On the back of each page from your ideal room, work with your partner to write a quality God has that also makes him a refuge for you when you feel like running away from life. For example, on the other side of a phone picture, you might write, "God is always ready to listen to me."**

Have partners share both sides of their pages with the rest of the group. Then ask the following questions.

discussion questions

- Was it easy to compare God to your ideal room? Why or why not?
- How is thinking about your ideal room like thinking about running away? about running to God?
- How has God been a refuge for you when you feel like running away?
- How does knowing that God is always ready to listen help you to feel better about facing the problems in your life?

☞Come as You Are

> **TOPIC:** Unity
> **THE POINT:** You can be part of Christ's body, the Church.
> **TIME:** 10 to 15 minutes

Have kids form a circle. Say: **Your job is to create a machine using each person here as an integral part of it. The only rule is that you must find an essential role in the machine for each person here. For example, if you choose to be a fan, four people could be fan blades while one might be an on-off switch and another might be a power cord. Once you've decided what machine to become, form it and show it in action.**

If you have more than ten students, consider having kids form smaller groups, and have each group create its own machine.

Once the group has created its machine, have kids show the machine in action. Then have kids form trios to discuss the following questions.

discussion questions

● What was it like to work together on this activity?

● How is the way you each had an essential role in the machine like how you can be part of Christ's body, the Church?

● Did you enjoy your role? Why or why not?

● How is the way you felt about your role in the machine like how you feel about your role in your circle of friends? in your family? in the church?

● What's one thing you've learned through this activity about belonging? about fulfilling your role in the church?

☞I.D. Required

TOPIC: Unity
THE POINT: God's people aren't perfect.
TIME: 10 to 15 minutes

Give each person an index card. Ask kids to jot down as many labels as they can to describe themselves. For example, an adult volunteer might be an "Asian, middle-class, Christian, college-educated, nonsmoking, right-handed, Republican, nearsighted, rural-born middle child of non-Christian parents."

Collect the cards, shuffle them, and read a few aloud. Have kids race to identify within ten seconds the person who wrote each card. Once everyone has been identified, have kids form pairs and discuss these questions:

discussion questions

● How did it feel to reduce yourself to labels?
● Do you ever do that to others in terms of race? age? religion?
● Why do people label each other?
● What's your least favorite (but accurate) label? most favorite?
● Why do some people enjoy being labeled?
● Do you think churches should be labeled? Why or why not?
● Since God's people aren't perfect, do we need labels to protect ourselves from each other? Why or why not?

Topical Index

Evaluation of
Group's Best Discussion Launchers for Youth Ministry

Please help Group Publishing, Inc., continue to provide innovative and usable resources for ministry by taking a moment to fill out and send us this evaluation. Thanks!

● ● ●

1. As a whole, this book has been (circle one):

Not much help   Very helpful

1   2   3   4   5   6   7   8   9   10

2. The things I liked best about this book were:

3. This book could be improved by:

4. One thing I'll do differently because of this book is:

5. Optional Information:

Name_____

Street Address _____

City_____State _____ Zip_____

Phone Number _____ Date_____

Give Your Teenagers a Solid Faith Foundation That Lasts a Lifetime!

Here are the *essentials* of the Christian life—core values teenagers *must* believe to make good decisions now...and build an *unshakable* lifelong faith. Developed by youth workers like you...field-tested with *real* youth groups in *real* churches...here's the meat your kids *must* have to grow spiritually—presented in a fun, involving way! Each 4-session, **Core Belief Bible Study Series** book lets you easily...

● Lead deep, compelling, *relevant* discussions your kids won't want to miss...

● Involve teenagers in exploring life-changing truths...

● Ground your teenagers in God's Word...and

● Help kids create healthy relationships with each other—and you!

Core Belief Bible Study Series lessons are flexible...and simple, step-by-step directions make leading your group easy whether you're a veteran youth worker or a first-time volunteer! Pick and choose which core beliefs your teenagers most need to explore! Each 4-session book is all you need for any size group!

Here are the Core Belief Bible Study Series titles already available...

Senior High Studies

Why **Being a Christian** Matters	ISBN 0-7644-0883-6
Why **God** Matters	ISBN 0-7644-0874-7
Why **Jesus Christ** Matters	ISBN 0-7644-0875-5
Why **Suffering** Matters	ISBN 0-7644-0879-8
Why the **Bible** Matters	ISBN 0-7644-0882-8
Why the **Holy Spirit** Matters	ISBN 0-7644-0876-3

Junior High/Middle School Studies

The Truth About **Being a Christian**	ISBN 0-7644-0859-3
The Truth About **God**	ISBN 0-7644-0850-X
The Truth About **Jesus Christ**	ISBN 0-7644-0851-8
The Truth About **Suffering**	ISBN 0-7644-0855-0
The Truth About the **Bible**	ISBN 0-7644-0858-5
The Truth About the **Holy Spirit**	ISBN 0-7644-0852-6

Order today from your local Christian bookstore, or write: Group Publishing, P.O. Box 485, Loveland, CO 80539.